Biblioteka
POEZIJA

Izdavač:
Sunčani breg, Beograd

1. izdanje

Urednik:
Dr Milutin Đuričković

Recenzent:
Dr Predrag Jašović

Naslovna strana:
Agsandrew

Stražnja stranica
Bruce Rolff

Štampa:
„Gora", Beograd

Z. M. Wise

THE PLEASANT DREAMERS: A NONLINEAR EPIC

Belgrade
2023

Acknowledgements

"Dreamland" was published in *Feminine Collective*

"The Perfect Reverie" was published in *Feminine Collective*

"Dream #8: Familiar Silhouette Scents" was published in *Feminine Collective*

"Jade" was published in *Setu Mag (Western Voices 2022)*

"Ballad of Jade and Alastair" was published in *Setu Mag (Western Voices 2022)*

THE FALLING CONTENTS

"Day comes,
And the brightness
Is hidden around me.
Shadows cover the light,
Drape it in sandstorms.
My beautiful mouth knows only confusion.
Even my sex is dust."

– Enheduanna, *from The Hymn to Inanna*
(translated by Jane Hirshfield)

To my mother, who is walking proof that optimism and perseverance (in dreams and in waking) pay off in the bittersweet end.

To my father, who always wished me goodnight and 'pleasant dreamers' before slumber.

FALLING ON THE SLEEP

In the tundra of the Echoing Deep,
the Awakers scream for cloying comfort,
for the conscious world regurgitates them out.

In the mountains of the Saintly Moon,
the Awakers make love to their shadows,
ejaculating starlight and aquatic reflections.

In the bogs of Voodoo Planets,
the Awakers resurrect the sixth (common) sense,
dancing away in the muck before the dawn's cantata.

In the cities of Midwestern Heaven,
the Awakers thrive with their sulfuric acid hearts,
melting infatuation purposes from the inside out.

Cursed Creeper,
Harmonious Quaker,
Amusing Sleeper,
Traumatic Awaker,
Fire Leaper,
Water Shaker…

Succumbing to the Queen,
no astral bodies remain to be seen.
Riding on a silverback equine to the other side,
meeting where the infant constellations collide.

Shearing the blanket wool off of the backs
of catatonic sheep,
deprivation eyelids shut and we are falling on the sleep.

June 3, 2018

DREAMLAND

Cast away into mystic mind oceans deep,
enter serene cerulean blue subconscious soul.
Sink into quicksand, remains of the Cultivator
of Sleep Production.
Slip away with the wind's best friend.
Soulless green plateau flatland rises,
mountain guardians defend their holy mooneyes.
Tactful window eyes view the other side,
a melting mirage of cities in the sky.
Take this shifting constellation hand,
for we must away into the epicenter of Dreamland.

February 1, 2018

THE NOT SO LONESOME DEATH OF THE SANDMAN

He assisted the reassurance process
with his soothing speech and only
takes on forms that individuals would understand,
singing lullabies before tone deaf audiences,
falling into slumber under waves of comprehension.

Regulation of time,
regulation of seasons.

He transformed sleepers into immortal Dreamers,
craving night sky flights towards ambition.

He had Dreamers to attend to,
pleasant and children with hunger for education.

He made the bad system men disappear
into thin, poisonous air before their very eyes.
They choked on the bile of immorality.
They choked on the saliva of regretful statements,
and then away'd into nothingness.

His vulnerability falters before the Digital Age,
succumbing to technological release.
Simonize naturality and become one with the screen.

But, he was a man, disintegrating
in front of his particle subjects,

divine painkilling people under the
guise of secular substance.
Fall under the quick beckon of shoreline fingers.

His existence since time immemorial,
engraved under every loving tree vow.
He cared not for recognition, for incognito
was his middle and final name.

Born into poverty in empty stars,
he spoiled himself with the riches of
satisfactory smiles from the factory floor.

From fornication to incubation,
from procreation to suspended animation.
He aided in the matchmaking rituals,
drawing better halves towards one another.

They paid their diurnal dues for two
tickets to love in an unconscious heartbeat.
They kissed before him without even thinking,
for they had met destiny, so what else was there?

He breathed on the necks of artists,
making their canvases vibrate violently,
enriching their notebooks with zest,
filling their studios with enticing sound,
weaving their fabric out of sheet color.

But, he was a man, viewing the lights,
watching his loved ones cry one last time
before his coarse figure became
microscopic puzzle pieces in the wind,
surrounding *familia* with his tranquil love.

December 10, 2017

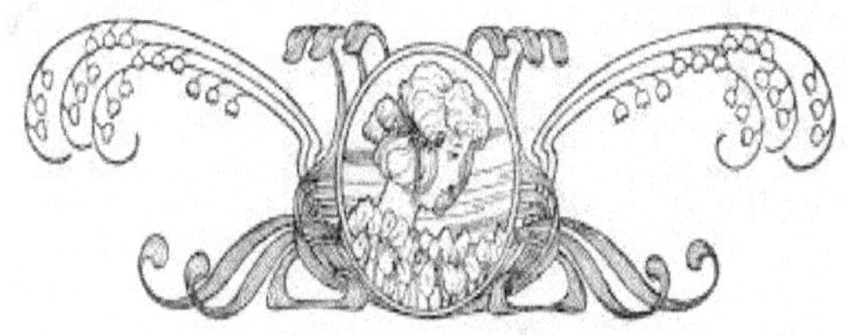

QUEEN OF DREAMS

Spectacled honeysuckle of knowledge,
we yield to you and your effortless
guidance and unbridled direction that
our star wall bodies may cross over to.

You speak your mind like a queen,
stepping out from a midsummer night's vault.
We greeted one another with hands
at a scene like this, preparing for
mystical pools of evening delights.

She forgot the rating system,
so the heart rate increases when her
forbidden portals open to a hungry seeker.

Welcome peril,
welcome risk,
tumble down adventures,
twirl with natural disasters,
I see her progression in weird orange lights.

Tickles my fancy and a random plethora.
Theater plays most elusive flashbacks.

Black is a shade, not a color.
Do sharks become human while consuming
the spirit of biped teeth?

Will the Queen of Dreams
kindly state her name before morning?

She covers me in planet rings.
She kisses me with lips of laughter.
She lets me listen to her insight of brilliance.

I slip into sheltered comfort,
the kind children of ages look to.
Why revert to prepubescence?
Sample of innocence becomes me.

I know nothing of limited time.
The body's button shrinks and the
heart grows, exposed to the lack of lessons.

A stampede scampers off when
right at home pressed lips against
hers, the lips that covered her Hispanic face.

I see myself dancing in a fire
that cannot be put out by humanity.
I see myself encased in artistic statues
that cannot be unmade by the creator.

Allow time for meditation to seep through
flesh wound, internal scar,
stay tuned and discover where we are.

Glorifying death in the centuries
zooming by on aeroplanes of war,
zero, she flies into no person's land.
Heavens help the lady with no direction.
The transition was never simple.

Will the Queen of Dreams
kindly make me hers before nightfall?

March 11, 2018

CHAI PRIESTESS AND THE DREAMLINERS

Cracked in two, corners divided,
fatalities evaded by the numbers,
the Dreamliners strike with carnage on their minds.

Call and answer, the third of the brains
remain sensible in personal journeys.

Back from the Battle of Addiction Island,
they fought with substance and speed.
Blurring together, these memories
are but lost fragments that erased themselves in
the Forbidden Archive, tiresome misdeeds.

Cascading along emerald tides,
the Dreamliners meditate with
foreign om tunes bursting with pages of
scandalous text, the classic option to alternative thinking.

Elder member at a café, sitting in
contemplation over internal wars.
When will they cease fire?
When will this underwater glass house
succumb to pressure below submarine depths?

Drinking the flowers of stagnation,
lemon-kissed stagnation,
and She rises, rises, rises from
subliminal message within the leaves of his last cup.

Drenched in bronze honey, grand exit,
speaks words of sweet gibberish.

"I am scripture in the flesh,
flying from Eastern wind influence.
Dreamliners, come to my chambers!"
And they levitate without hesitation.

Her aura's doing, vibrating, humming anxiety songs,
gushing with star power from above.

Burning through picture frames of mind,
the Chai Priestess consumes the
boiling volcanic temperature she wishes.

Want to be here, get away, get high,
balloon of hot air, lift her proclamation.
She gives her signature sermon on every mount.

"I am the afterglow after climax,
prophetic puppet on the strings of fate.
My puppeteer lives behind the nooks and crannies of
our full ivory sphere mistress,
the one who turns us wild."

Seminal speech chooses the most unfit,
survival of the perfectly sane in absolutes.
Saintly misfortune arrows land on the
hunchbacked, starry-eyed descendant.

Marcus, the Dumbfounded Imp,
tiresome of his grief-stricken colony.
Marks liquid territory on mutiny's throne.

January 21, 2018

JADE

A girl, almost woman, complete hallucination,
born of prophet visions and dancing on windows.

Mug of rosewater and hibiscus tea until she was 23.
She messed with the minds of mystics and gryphons,
humans in the real world questioned her ever motive,
for their dreams belonged to her guidance and direction.

Caramel beauty from head to toe leaving no straight lines,
pathway of curves became her in a matter of seconds.
One non-objectifying gaze into her spiritual spheres and the
self-direction is made quite clear for the folk who gather
here.

Sunday of silence for her lips of spur-of-the-moment speech,
for she feels her words are more concrete on parchment.
Monday, she teaches the young minds, wrapping futuristic
ideas
around feline yarn globes, unmade and unwound.
She never fails to entertain the easily amused.

Tuesday, she composes concertos in her magnificent head,
playing them before every stuck up musical committee.
Wednesday, she dedicates time lapses to dreamers in
poverty,
no dreaming child left behind to choke on the reality's
dystopian dust.

Thursday of darkness, Great Goddess Moon never
shows her face,
La Llarona weeps in the pitch black midnight hour by
a secret river.
Friday, she meets a heart-eyed customer as her role of the
banker of dreams.
He cannot believe she said affirmative with a smile to his
question of courtship.

Saturday for the sake of creation!
Saturday for the sake of manifestation!

This life of the lack of control and independence seemed
unfair
until she laid right side up on the oddly-worded sentences
of Alastair.

April 12, 2018

ALASTAIR

On a steel nightstand, his notebooks once lay.
A person, a poet, a pauper, a chained heart beyond repair.
He keeps his literary treasures close to a lover's cheek kiss of comfort.
No one dares to touch the classic works of Voltaire.

Under mortar and stone, born from the ashes of his avian mother.
Negotiation with warlocks, insemination by the act of some strange affair.
Accepting oxygen as his first love, he dines on the thirst of inhalation.
No one dares to stare into the hopeful eyes of Baby Alastair.

Adolescence becomes him, for his suburban hands smell like labor.
His heart is still a potion of purity, an organ free of all cares.
Never any blood rush to his mind, for all hypotheses form below.
No one dares to climb the hellish hills of heavenly hope with Alastair.

Around the Mountains of Impertinence, existentialism becomes his middle name.
Stolen identity, losing faith, this caring lad forms a nom de guerre.
A hermit resting on plateaus flatter than this paper drafts.

No one dares to kill the objective of time with Alastair.

Through the battles of obligation, he served his country
so numb.
Blinded by the killing pleasures, deafened by the bangs of
warfare.
Every item of military assault, melted to make the bridges
of protested crossing.
No one dares to interrupt the peacemaking progress
of Alastair.

Inside the willow branch casket, his two faces of light shone
in the other direction.
A premature ending to a journeyed life of optimism sank
into despair.
He holds no regrets, for his generation has always passed
on younger than eggs.
No one dares to join in the merriment with the laughing
corpse of Alastair.

Restless on the other side, hovering from portal to portal.
Even the village of skeptics warn the living to beware.
An insatiable starvation occurs within the pit of his
transparent stomach.
No one dares to indulge the ravings of the starving ghost
of Alastair.

Praise to the psyche, for the purgatorial trial has concluded!
"Make me a Dreamer so pleasant, to free the caged minds everywhere!"
And so the last wish was granted by the Spectacled Queen Before Time.
No one dares to lead the Pleasant Dreamers towards egalitarianism without Alastair.

April 12, 2018

PLEASANT DREAMERS

Lords and ladies of the puzzled minds…
this is their eldest world.
Old wives tales spin themselves.
Husband legends weave the fabric
ripped from the shaken senior hands of time.
They stay disorganized on today's bookshelves.
Pleasant Dreamers cling to Mother Nature's portal.
Pleasant dreams to all who seek to be immortal.

Slumbering to escape half of morality's grasp,
the populace who clench their tentacles 'round the
conscious.
Human psyches will not settle for anything less.
Morphing biology, the rearranging of bones
to the beat of the perfect andante
leaves no trace behind for the new human dying to confess.
Pleasant Dreamers, protectors of those who sleep unaware.
Pleasant dreams to the ancestral nightmares.

Horrors waver in on a ghostly ship of crystal,
full of a hull of fools haunting in
half-witted melodies composed for the lyrically blind.
Raven-haired maiden of brown skin shows
true virtues in the darkest hours of her daring vocals.
Nights divided by inconsequential advocates of womankind.
Pleasant Dreamers leap into the bounty of stars to take flight.
Pleasant dreams and a most elegant goodnight.

Sailing far away from voyages to
isles of deepest concentration,
the Pleasant Dreamers chart conclusive territory.
Turning fable into factual folly,
molding nudity into nubile news,
the Pleasant Dreamers are amused by their favorite allegory.
Mystical beings of green,
narrating every afterhours scene.

Captain A leads the civilized ranks
to the median between destiny and mutiny,
but the Pleasant Dreamers sketch the skies as spirit
designers.
Traitor M has mutilated the Chai Priestess,
for lustful desire and claim to her herbal throne,
but the Pleasant Dreamers clash with the Dreamliners.
Rivalry for the laborious acts of treason,
polluting the multicolored clouds of every season.

Never worry about eventuality's cocoon,
bursting with evolution and uncanny resemblance,
for the Pleasant Dreamers accept every protégé.
Never fear the peaceful flickers of light
or the peaceful truce of darkness,
for the Pleasant Dreamers guard the sacred passageway.
All of humanity's equality reigns supreme.
Insanity's gods only know how this started out as an
innocent dream.

November 21, 2017

DREAM OF CONSCIOUSNESS

Somewhere else places us here
among Blake's elderly starry pole.
Losing control of senses old and rediscovered,
we slip into uncharted waters.
We cannot believe the words
told by Victorian murder schemes,
elaborately sung in blood-curdling romantic screams.
"This…is…not…"

Sailing on oceans of fire, treacherous flames,
pining for the bittersweet escape.
We can almost taste penetrative exploration.
Beneath our lips lies hordes of
dark matter secrets that claim the
souls of last year's sacrificial celebration.
"This…is…not…"

Never awake long enough to be reborn in an
immortal body of immobility.
Never slumbering long enough to
reach full conscious potential of the next day.
Still weep under willow heads and
wish upon dandelion wine glasses.
Still sleep on pillow beds and
dish out pickup lines to the masses.
"This is not real life."

January 31, 2018

THE PERFECT REVERIE

We wandered once in this Zen garden,
absorbing every color of sound we
could hear with synesthesia as our guide.
Twin flames were put out by the
electric ocean we conducted out of
thin air sighs, synchronizing with the
galloping stampede…gliding through wind without cares.
We wandered, but only once.

We recited our written manifestations to one another,
connecting with the collective creativity as
two self-educated academics with a thirst for literature.
Unread palms enter psychic phenomena,
lavender with twists of violet.
I have voluntarily stepped into your web of seduction,
Arachnid Mistress.
Tangle me in each verse, in each stanza.
We recited, but only once.

We kissed until the two spheres who
battled for 24 hour custody of the sky.
Our goddesses and legends have entered into myth.
Keeping our tasteful lips at an unrestricted distance,
but when we have reached nirvana's wink
it hardly seems to matter anymore.
Daydream believers, we pay tribute to you.
We kissed, but only repeatedly.

All of your hearts have seemed to
stop beating, remaining idle on the darkest side.
Dires that never pass, the flames of war,
sweep themselves under shielded rugs
on National Wealth's regretful floors.
All prior scribblings left as etchings on
French caves, signs of upright life in
simplicity's downward spiral gatherings.

Grandfathered into this burning meadow,
a scene as bland as chaos itself.
We dance the *cumbia* like you taught me.
Your Spanish eyes smile wider than these arms can
hold you.
Not ready to grieve you just yet,
we enter one final death trek into
abandoned sanctuary, vandalized halls of monarchs.
Knock three times, my rolling tongue mistress of insecurities.

We loved one another until subcontinents told nature to
divide us in the least amicable way.
Left to colonize in a haven of barbaric mannerisms,
we sink our teeth into carnal flesh,
feeding primal instincts to provide imagery for the hours
of tonight.
The woman of every dawn dines in her birth gown,
awaiting further life instructions from below the surface.
We loved, but only for every lifetime.

December 11, 2017

CLOSING EYES, OPENING COLOURS

Tightly wound, shut out to the
landscape portraits beyond the screen.

People will sing sea chanties to their
ancestors draped in fog, lurching terrors.
Fell from aloft, second glances.

Their advances placed in second.
Kings of the wood sell themselves
for the kindling of martyrdom.

Natural selection at its most pitiful,
fitting of the survivalists…

Closing eyes,
opening colours.

Working for the angels beneath the lids,
wings of fatality lap about in constant
mysterious bouts o ingenuity.

Wildflower bursts, moving in time,
caged to the limited descension.

Fireflies, polychromatic and unified,
congregate to witness this candlelit
moment… porcelain teeth chatter.

Mannequins animate and take life.
Enter and exit the feelings of oblivion.

Closing eyes,
opening unconscious cinema.

December 11, 2017

ALASTAIR CORELLIUS AND THE PLEASANT DREAMERS

Alastair, a stunned lad of twenty-eight,
confesses to no higher power but his own.
In his euphoric realm, nothing is as it seems.
Alastair could lead them all to their soul mates,
locking lips of moisture and eyes as firm as bones,
wishing them a heartfelt goodnight and pleasant dreams.

Who are the Dreamers?
Figments of imaginative reality,
Callers of the Almighty Shield.
Why are they Dreamers?
Plentiful purposes in a war of star door games,
taking up chuckling arms in a humorous battlefield.

A band of tree-hugging pacifists,
violence never entered the brains of these free
speech blasphemers.
Viewers and architects of the hovering mountains,
lightning riders and thunder rollers welcome the Pleasant
Dreamers.

Here they come to turn myth into legend,
a chimaera orgy of tales to ascend.
Epics read from *Ramayana* to *Kalevala,*
meditation made around the circumference of a mandala.

A shadow of a voice entangled with silvery hair,
glows as brightly as a shimmering jewel so rare.
Jade, they named her after the Queen Maiden Faire.
Independent and protected under the watchful eye
of Alastair.

Alastair, slender and a tragic fellow,
buried in the tombs of his pages turning on the highest self,
well-read and an unwritten future.
Alastair preferred the activists of the mellow,
chanting om words to contact his higher self.
Leaves every verbal document with a kissing signature.

What are the Dreamers?
Faithful to the land and their Queen,
a chocolate-dipped, Sun-hugged lady of fire.
How are they Dreamers?
Granted by the trials endured in catatonic success,
persons of choice to follow the dialogues that transpire.

Cooled off by electricity flames,
the meek, inherent redeemers.
Passionate and wild beyond their millennia,
thank the ancient balance for the Pleasant Dreamers.

Sequences of Spanish beauty playing castanets,
asking her to dance to the rhythm of a series of minuets.
Leaving behind flowery mementos on the Royal Doorpost,
everyone existent is a purposeful ghost.

Never the case of looking worse for wear,
using the looks of ocean seduction ensnare.
Once a human with the tendencies of former earthen care,
kept hidden betwixt the foremost poems of the last Dreamer Alastair.

November 21, 2017

DREAM WOMAN

Hazel eyes blink into the deep existence,
body as caramel as the flow of consciousness streams.
ASMR voice makes the most innocent shudder into
nothingness,
hands as civil as her pacifist warlord mind.
Silk hair extends to connect the stillborn stars,
lips as indigo as the remedy of tea flowers during
ill exhaustion.
Not as dream goddess,
but person of absolute astral waves.
Dream Woman, appearing only after darkness's curtain falls
to the soil,
and the Dreamer pleasantly grins as the sunshine greets his
waking vision.

March 8, 2018

ALASTAIR AND THE CELESTIAL LAIR

Secret states of mind rest in his nocturnal claws.
Panther eyes of veil-piercing gold see through all.
To raise the wild in civilization is to reach into the archives.
Reverting to the all familiar fetal state in search of treasure.
He found treasure troves of literary masterpieces in the
Celestial Lair.

One sun child burns for repeated failure but rises
to lead the revolution into total peaceful blackness.
It is the only way to see when shame takes hold of
the guilty eyes, wandering about as a futile source
of distraction.
He found moon children dancing on the strands of his
corkscrew Bolan hair.

Following the rats of Eliot and the harpies of Sexton,
he tiptoes on the ghazals of Ghalib, settling in the eclectic
nature of Tagore.
To raise the dead among the living is to reach into the graves
never letting go of the skeletal hands of allies walking side
by side as equals.
He found the most sacred mausoleum, vandalized by the
March Hare.

Age-old knowledge comes once in a blue star,
planetary shot.
It glows as bright as a functional family,
yearning for happier occasions and earlier times.

Everything learned, factual opinions and opinionated facts.
He found the wisdom of his grandfather in the seat of his glazed rocking armchair.

Severed ties with the ancient texts,
severed connections with all outside worlds,
severed heads laugh at every attempt to shut out 'no'.
Severed the rest of disposable parasites until solitude means yes.
He found nothing but a future reflection of himself in the Celestial Lair.

BALLAD OF JADE AND ALASTAIR

Two ordinary Dreamers without fantasizing of light lead
lives of mediocrity,
independent opinions without the basis of fact chose
to murder modern society.
One fulfills the routine of pity party, swimming in leftover
streams of rainwater,
one indulges in the occasional nightmare films, playing
before the annual slaughter.
Coming together to seek the answers by way of boisterous
laughter,
they mesmerize and hypnotize one another in the endeavor
of unintentional disaster.
Hushed by their own fingers of mutual commonality,
two moon-kissed slices of Dutch apple pie care not about
nationality.

Spending holidays in the Sun during crucial times
of unprovoked war,
their petty problems were pretty vacant near the starry shore
and watery floor.
Preferring the devices of the simple past to failing advanced
modernity,
their noses were stuck in the books written beyond eternity.
One consumed rosehips and hibiscus, the other sank under
the River Darjeeling.
Repelled by skepticism, they give in to the Chief of Feelings.
Queen of Dreams played cherubic arrow owner of the
Cosmos.

Craving more emotional affection, they care not if they overdose.

Jade, Lady Logic and artiste in her own musical delight,
she dances like a priestess under the influence of Druid sights.
Every idea for experimental sounds causes an explosion towards the inconceivable.
Soothing the protesting voices in her head, they insist on controlling the unbelievable.
Rejected by auditory organizations of pomposity, deeming her work derivative.
Outsmarting them in hush tones, she reigns as Princess of the Imaginative.
Always the woman of independence who remained dedicated and headstrong.
His essence entered hers beneath the harmonious melodies in perfect song.

Alastair, fairest fellow and bard of his own expanded mind,
struggling to preserve the tremored hands and praying tongues of humankind.
Taking on the guise of a peace-offering pacifist with ironic weaponry,
his intentions were purer than the authority on everything contradictory.
First love married to creation, faceless girl who provided the sensational seeds.
His copious stacks of written works concocted in unspeakable durations of speed.

Hearing about the rumors of 'passionate love' in gossiping romance tomes,
a maiden of legend came to life in between the lines of his first poem.

So, a divine union of indescribable measures was made.
"Bound by no deity but our own words in the common tongue,"
spoke the articulate mouth of Jade.
An infinite number of lifetimes they will forever share.
Strolling hand in hand, two lovers walk on air,
the Gemstone Lady and her Alastair.

April 12, 2018

THE PLEASANT DREAMERS

Crossing the portals of surrealism,
all existent light forms change shapes.
Happy go-lucky personas swift eagle transformation,
feeling oneself expanding wingspan.

Soaring above rooftops, they can see
star bright, the Northern King on his perch.

They are the reason they live tonight.
They live for the night and dine on the day.
They dine on the Celadon apples of the Moon
and turn sour voice elixir into saltwater ambrosia.

They all have egos to court and make love with.
In and out of sorts, facing belly up.
Nothing blocks them from creation but themselves.

Escape into next month's autumn dreamscape,
a reprieve from reality's checks and balances.

Thought they remembered their ancient allies,
scribblings of unconscious renderings.
The art of slumber is the path way to endless hopes.

Neither here for glory nor greed but the
hardship of priceless fortunes, spoken through

printed lips of libel, the letters burn in
envelope casing, messages drowning in oceans of fire.

Across the interwoven barriers,
the Pleasant Dreamers enter still vibrancy.

Careful castle mountains part the way
for evening wind shadows, rustling with every
step they take, outlining silhouettes.

Duet between Alastair and his fair lady,
romping in billows of clouds, wordless choral vocals
echo and pierce veils beyond understanding.
He could never understand her electric physique,
the way she struck him during storms of passion.

Changing faces in midsentence, followers rise from
jigsaw puzzle ashes, reincarnation of confusion.
Roaming the land his faith in no above,
colors merge and sounds ignite for the
fourth movement in his head, oh, orchestral delight!

They desire not to remain in marshland valleys.
Travel in sequence towards the outer rim,
celestial seasonings to garnish the meat of minds.

Help them reform and refine nightmarish
games of abuse, the unwanted physical hands
wither away, fiendish swine of her traumatic half!

She remains still, shaken…stir crazy.
They grant her warrior status, unbreakable
maiden of metal arising from her doldrums.

Appearing to whisper secretive cameo words,
The Pleasant Dreamers exit orgasmic disaster.

November 21, 2017

DREAM(ER)

Awoke to the wind beneath the wings of a Pterodactyl,
chewing on the last of prehistoric milkweed.
Its companion, lacking ears, attempts to lip read.
Sacrificial amputee, the legs of Holy Mother Centipede,
placing each appendage into a charitable satchel.

Nightmarish warnings of the Northwest,
Logical Queen hides in the armor behind her soul.
Putting one hand on the silken bookmark and the other
on her breast.
Ascending to interstellar dimensions, she spaghettifies
in this wormhole.

Making little sense from the fragmented phrases of Freud,
he slips into the Egyptian comfort of Ozymandias
whilst listening to a Grecian intrada by Amadeus.
Take us forward to experimental instrumentals of Barrett's
Floyd.
Drug-laden journey of the troubled fellow Rael,
forced to endure the tales of one's candid past.
In the end, he became no one's iconoclast,
so his morals drowned moments after setting sail.
Hatched from this metal cocoon,
awakened by the sapphire gleaming of selective runes.

Awoke to the theatrical screech of a Pteranodon,
amused by the animated dance of the mannequins,
played on an out of tune Viennese violin.

Yet again, model marble has been demoted to porcelain.
Interrupt not the sequencing of inducing Kublai Khan.

April 29, 2018

DREAMLINER

Sipping on teasing samples of Pink Moscato,
the jingoist believes himself to be a Shriner.
Iconoclast breaking operatic rhythm in plain staccato,
playing for an audience of one as a struggling headliner.

He leads a gullible group for a failing expedition
to converse with Star Bear Ursa Minor.
On the way up the wrecking avalanche, a brief intermission.
A recruit brought him to a royal cult as a Dreamliner.
It takes no minute speck of intellection
to perform a black magic woman resurrection.
Brought back into the world of infantile nudism,
leading the revolutionaries into a scene of skinless activism.

Automatically found as a servant for a clampdown
in the lushest region of space, turned two-faced moonshiner.
"I would return to the haven of my hometown,
to plant my birthplace roots if matters were finer."
During times when compartmentalism was serious
turned into his duration in a white-dipped room delirious.
Lifting heavy hopes from his breast of fogbank nights,
he takes a kamikaze chance in telling her a one-liner.
Once a lord of mortality, now a measly arthropodic parasite.
Bring back the original globe designer.

Never perceived as the Great Diviner.
Just a blind trend follower of the Dreamliners.

PLEASANT(LY) DREAM(ING) BLUES

Fell asleep this morning
after a night of lucid dreaming.
Fell asleep this morning
after a night of lucid dreaming.
I ignored the previous warnings
before the sunlight started streaming.

Going back to the Waters of Ignorance,
the time of unhinged philosophy.
Going back to the Waters of Ignorance,
the time of unhinged philosophy.
The wilderness removed my innocence,
leaving me as a child for the wild geography.

Intellectual dialogues for cranial ejaculation,
kissing the many minds of Her, my main fixation.
Pleasant dreams to the blues,
pleasant dreams to you.

Watching the futuristic cavalcade,
one rebel dancer steps forward to promenade.
Pleasant dreams of the blues,
pleasant dreams of you.

Awake from a sleep paralysis coma,
he awakens to her natural aroma.
Pleasantly dreaming of the blues,

pleasantly dreaming of you.

Started slumbering as a self-declared king,
but woke up to the realization of a peasant.
Started slumbering as a self-declared king,
but woke up to the realization of a peasant.
Witnessed a Venus fly trap's meal sing,
disguised as a dreamer who was never pleasant.

Thinking not with the brains, but with the phallus,
with the logic of a catatonic shoe shiner.
Thinking not with the brains, but with the phallus,
with the logic of a catatonic shoe shiner.
I never wished to encounter Marcus
and his band of merry Dreamliners.

Eight straight hours of Eastern meditation,
the best form of alternative medication.
Pleasant dreams to the blues,
pleasant dreams to you.

Cuddling her until the conclusion of the weekend,
evolution of love dissolves, yet struggles to pretend.
Pleasant dreams of the blues,
pleasant dreams of you.

I have returned to your pair of affectionate arms,
your laughter in moonlight, your softhearted charms.
Pleasantly dreaming of the blues,
pleasantly dreaming of you.

DANCE OF THE PLEASANT DREAMERS

We have possessed the power,
the power to stand on solid clouds.
Since kingdom come, their fog sheets enshroud
where the sweetest sweat has turned sour,
raining upon jagged foundations on the Sapphire Tower.

Where Dreamers and Dreamliners come together,
a forbidden unity that breaks the ice of taboo.
See them congregating nervously in the opal ballroom,
an eager blend of diversity, an impromptu rendezvous.

Attempting to serenade *senorita* once more,
playing dulcet tones for her on the Spanish guitar.
May we have this dance with the
one who converses with the stars?

She lights the floor ablaze.
With feet of flames, she commands.
A solo act for all to see in awe!
She dazzles the spectator with disastrous demand.
Operatic in voice, her sound travels,
yet refuses to stand perfectly still.
All eyes on her faltering ways,
sensing her wind-up copycat spinning on the windowsill.

Tormented by the asylum of screamers,
we have gathered here to rid ourselves of all naysayers and
blasphemers.

Take our hands and dance *bachata* with the Pleasant Dreamers.

Unstructured dancers rush to the edge of midnight.
Bare feet touch the mirror floor of snow.
Liquid courage in the form of aged Merlot.
Tipsy feather shoes slur words to disunite,
making every beverage consumer a parasite.

Come into the room past the Queen's chambers,
quarters where the sleeping bards lie.
They have composed the perfect spoken melody,
secretive verses for their modus operandi.

Love has opened the door yet again,
a womb shield of flesh begins to procreate.
May we have this dance with the
one who hides in the eyelashes of his soul mate?

Alastair takes the hand of Jade,
the desert-kissed beauty of unconscious Earth.
Destined to make all ends meet for one another,
a decree made on a sacred tree from birth.
Marcus whistles tunes of encouragement,
daydreaming of all past lovers singing in A Minor.
By one single hand, he extends to a Dreamer on the end,
they turn away the subliminal animosity of the Dreamliners.

Tormented no more by the asylum of screamers,
we fed the beasts to an audience of naysayers and

blasphemers,
slow dancing to nothing with the Pleasant Dreamers.

January 12, 2018

DUST OF LUST

Taking turns for the best,
sleight of hand, magic efforts,
cards turn to ash, take me by surprise.

Bodies are under the spell, under the influence
yet again, lovely hormonal sleepers.
Seductive Sandwoman and strange drugs
at the ready, at the calling.

Blue cascading ice caves turn to
liquid white protein pools,
swallowing the children to sustain life.
She tasted of pineapple tropics tonight.

Giving herself over, goodbye pool and
hello to the transparent ocean,
gushing like a youthful fountain from
in between her self-professed definition of Heaven.

And how they shuddered when
pink met pink in deliberate contact.
Lips on her face met lips beneath,
kissing the idle flower bud with gusto.

In an instant, his music met hers.
Promiscuous muses of love, please
repeat this time loop of spiritual electricity.

I cannot take it!
She cannot take it!
I took her tonight.
She took me always.

Sparks of spice fill her room
with scented lightning flashes.
Her moans are thunder claps of satisfaction.

Oh, strike me again, lover from above!
Entwined in arachnid webs without witness,
we engage in nature's gift of perfection,
without binding rings and paper legality.
Oh, strike me again, tantric temptress!

We need not words to define our
prolonged purgatorial passion pit.
I stopped believing in streetlight people
the moment our independent banda song
played at full maximum volume.

Dime que me queres at the top of your lungs!
Stand at every corner and tell me
in your rolling tongue who your only one is.

O' Happy Notebook Pages, I cling
to you for guidance and wisdom!

Anticipation beating against my breast,
pump blood through the right organs

as she asks me to pump her gently.

I would rather be inside you, Spring Lover.
Our sailing vessels of flesh leave for home.
Inside you, I am forever home.

December 10, 2017

DREAM #8: FAMILIAR SILHOUETTE SCENTS

She is a cinnamon shadow,
outline of spice in her valleys below.
A shimmering smile of ten plagues
makes the atmosphere consistently vague.

Time pyramids shift into the sand of the escapades.
Conquests from the gossiping charade,
pissing out falsifying words of lemonade.
They lead their own illusory parade.

He is a little head of blood rushes,
blueprint of the mind home he unknowingly crushes.
A lad who plays fantasy roulette
winds up in a monthly tourniquet.

Here he has entered the Land of the Bizarre,
nostalgia for the rainbow attic of dust and guitars.
His eyes see red handprints on the soil of Mars.
Identity was stolen and forever lost in the scripture of stars.

And he will meet the guardian at dawn.
And he will be reborn as a silent, wandering fawn.

Turned on by the gown she wears,
this swan takes a dive in liquid gang waters,
an undersea battle from aquatic ages.
She cleanses herself of all past transgressions,
the cardinal sins of flights she has never taken,

eternally married to the wisdom of her avian sages.

In this world of pansexual polyamory,
the subconscious sweater wears everyone.
It loves every contact and silken touch,
indulging in tastes of sweetness of the highlight reel reruns.
It wraps like a python around its host.
Summer hell chases away its woolen interior,
leaving the stinging Sun to worship fabric ghosts.
Sailing and waving to cloud-kissed aeroplanes,
I can fly to the edge of the near-extinct planet.
I meet my Spanish lady on the other side and
smelling her neck, perfume *au naturale,*
listening to the sounds of cacophonous castanets.

We kissed once before in Andalucía,
teleporting to the jungles of Belize.
Malnourished from the island's healing curiosities,
a drink of pineapple water is enough to survive,
but none can replace the undying ache to please.

Coming in and out of this daze, no recollection.
Out of the womb, I emerge from the Cesarean section.
From this temporary body, I feel a slight disconnection,
half blind, half deceased, without any direction.

She is an amaryllis shadow,
tortured by the previous night's afterglow.

December 11, 2017

FACELESS SPIRITUAL ELECTRICITY

Your shadow has memorized this bed,
leaving impressions of hands gasping for air.
Your silence has been amplified,
vocals rolling their speech, the language of touch.
Who was it that your starlight form tried to ensnare?
Never ready for her human words, so I rely on your
silhouette as a crutch.

Life began in the heartbeat lands of Africa,
rising as steady warriors of the Sun.
They found more illustrious answers to life's questions,
sensing storms in savannahs nationwide.
Always pondering with regality being overrun,
remaining as equal and stable before the Great Divide.

From first contact to last sigh of exhaustion,
I can sense you moving through the dark.
Monochromatic lover, your schemes are never-ending,
for they bypass the blueprint and into the focus of your
birthmark.
Matriarch of sugar, sweep me up in your sweetness,
blissful cubes sparkling by the vines.
Bitter words counter heavenly actions,
making their way to the grandest design.

Life began in the shifting times of Africa,
but the lightning struck the center of simplicity.
Carnal pleasures are ours t share,

mutually entwined in faceless spiritual electricity.

"I can feel your body's entirety,
the lips of a merciful queen,
the breasts of liberating support.
We are lock and key of noble metals.
Gyrating, pulsating, enveloping ourselves
in the momentary lapses of beauty.
Dreamer's romance incarnate, the
other side of teasing circle kisses."
Life began in the silver sands of Africa,
morphing into your seductive persona.

I can feel myself within you,
fraction of humanity surrounded by your walls.
Welcome my presence, Great Wetness,
leading me to the castle of euphoric halls.
I damn myself on a whim, yet I
curse each moment of spasmed withdrawals.
Without the connection of your whisper'd soul,
you are just droplets, the taste of poisonous alcohol.
So, good evening to your galactic face yet again.
Until your unknown physique, I thought I had it all.

Life began in the ancestral songs of Africa,
reciting oral verses and past tales of unwanted toxicity.
Step out from your muted shroud and claim my soul,
so we can be
mutually engaged in faceless spiritual electricity.

DREAMING OF YOU IN ALL TIME ZONES

Dragging her ocean tail out from the shoreline foam,
chocolate mermaid from the hidden chapters of the tomes.
Formerly Queen of the Underwater City,
she feels no ounce of self-pity
when the worker drones lay waste to what she once
called home.

Happy Days to every draft she has rewritten.
Regaining her status as a humanoid stunt!
Little does she know her ancestor is on the prowl.
All at once, a poetic passerby becomes smitten.
Never before had he experienced such feelings on the hunt.
Roar to the left and let tonight's love howl.
Hand in palm, they obliviously admire local street art,
greeting each other before time's face demands they depart.

Thought every golden being was extinct,
let alone the brilliance of this grand fixation.
Leave us be and let love free, break away
from the cracked egos of concrete environment.
I will show her the sights of land,
a singing darkness under the influence of manifestation.
One more forlorn glance at the limestone cliff dive
before we reach the hours of bedroom retirement.

Based on the fraction of the moonlight that shone,
he dreamt of her in every time zone.

Back to the aquatic core of waterstone.

Confession conference for two in a condemned graveyard,
stroll down the broken-hearted boulevard.
Safe to say the misfits and outcasts we ridicule
are worth more on this ground than every minuscule
molecule,
for he was nothing more but her faithful bard.

Above these clouds, she was Queen of Regulated Feminism.
Her loyal subjects believed only in the subjective,
deaf to all attempts at a mind or lip reading.
Cultural growth of the classes celebrate universal mysticism.
She sends a message-kissed envelope to the night detective,
delivering it to her higher self before the dusk preceding.
Certainty is but a myth the authorities forbid,
sealed beneath the sands of a suburban pyramid.

Love is a poem that is written on your forehead,
words spoken as sweet as seasonal mango.
Lust is a driving force of magnets,
sparks flying as two bodies of drowning flesh collide.
Love is a dance to step to without music,
head between her thoughts, rose between the teeth in tango.
And time is but an irrelevant farce,
forcing us to make our own downfallen landslide.

Taking her by the hand, she leapt through a primitive
telephone,

confessing her love for him in every time zone.
Back to their home within the welcoming caves
of mountainstone.

January 11, 2018

HIGHLIGHT REEL OF THE EXAGGERATED QUARTER CENTURY AGES

Naked and screaming state of mind,
infancy boils milk formula, formulating
first words into chain link sentences.

Unconscious brain gases, cloud of curiosity,
stability on two feet, walking on apple cider.

Being facetious behind tiger masks,
can you see the other side where the
strings and cheek perspiration meet?

Put all Atlas weight on other burdens,
sinking below prioritization and become a
unicorn without its rightful horn,
a hornet without its rightful stinger,
a manta ray without its majestic momentum.

And we are all the beginning enders,
closing cases that have been tarnished,
playing subliminal messages on reversed scratched records.
Mother's hallway laugh, Father's galactic songs.

And we are the oddities who
creep politely around your success,
sobbing at the stories of deicide.
Kill a god with other gods.

Twenty-eight and still
cannot relate,
the masses have their grasses to graze,
sheeple on the steeple being set ablaze.

December 10, 2017

FULL HEAD OF EMPTY DREAMS

Three-headed wolf beckons to me
with human fingers and a serpent's hissing tongue.
It wraps me with viper coils and
tickles my fancy with jungle feline tail.
It tells me yarns in garbled underwater languages,
deciphered only through lucid riding.
"Deliverance is upon you,
decadent with a full head.
Your mind is chaos incarnate that even the
most superior demon would fear."

A somnambulist at heart walks on sleep,
kisses with the thirst of jaws,
embraces everything, yet clings to nothing.
Slip into serene depths, O' Wanderer,
revolving around planets as a
comatose lad in interstellar bliss.
The stars of illusory death predicted so.

Three-headed wolf whispers to me
seductive third party voices in near-perfect harmony.
Oh, Siren of Deceit, sing to me, my love!
Looked upon by shattering mirrors,
esteem of the self has hit an all time low.
"Come in to this elementary garden,
where the blossoms are aroused by your arrival
and presence."

No longer a pleaser for his own crowd,
a deity of vain reason exercises all vanity,
bleeding from the inside out, as instructed by no one.
Paradoxical fellow enters a picture frame,
a dreamer of pleasant expectations.
Born woman, destiny led to transitional manhood,
making names for his ever-increasing brains.

Fully evolved by midnight's stroke of the member,
his voice booms with sensibility, calling out
followers to believe the holy inevitable,
followers to redefine the impossible.

Links clinkity-clink on his chain of ethical command,
requiring no love in this lifetime or the next.
He finds it naturally with no effort,
music of the lyre to the breast of the player.
Notes surround the entirety of his being.
Thank this Dreamland and every other residing area.

Three-headed wolf nuzzles me in reassurance,
gliding beside me with dragonfly wings,
peering into my soul with manta ray's eyes,
keeping me close as an over-possessive panther.
Faces of neutral clowns, stone smiles of amusement.
"Setting of the forgetting Sun, the joker is wild.
You have not known bittersweet innocence dreaming like
that of a child."

December 17, 2017

PATTERNS

Colors merging, senses forming…
the dark, the light, the unfolding patterns.
One anti-heroine commanded to step forward and
wear the icy committed rings of Saturn.

She has loved herself before…
constantly being regurgitated to the reject shore.

Outcasts from bottom lines to top marks,
they call upon the Elders of Evolution.
This is recurring, a haunting torture,
forever bound to the impoverished chains of destitution.

Sounds echoing, lines collapsing…
the voices, the messages, the unrehearsed songs.
One villain turns over a new leaf,
incinerating blueprints and sipping cups of oolong.

Steeds from the next land over moving with stiff haste,
suitors near and far long for her taste,
forever bound to the belt of the chaste.

Shapes assembling, walls crumbling…
the angles, the diagrams, the dimensions.
One repeating film plays yet again,
wearing out the paradoxical mind extensions.

Protected by the eggshells of Mother Hen,
seldom see at the asylum yet again,
yearning for a tale of untold Zen.

January 12, 2018

READING THE STARLIGHT PALMS

Backward lines read in reverse after
stepping out from the other side of an antique mirror
with a head of metal and hair from a '69'd summer,
they read the starlight palms
to regain clarity of what occurred
last millennium and the eight days preceding.

Drank forest rainwater from the
mud cement pawprint and he became
lunar beast of carnage-filled list.
And how we sprinted towards the
ever-present full of the half moon.
Awake, I wonder what time it is.

Forward lines rise like the hair on arms,
peach fuzz surrounded by goose bumps, a result of
her touch and rainbow response, we are
riders who switch fighter/lover stances,
only to share a mutual maelstrom of pleasure.
Awake, I clean the stained protein sheets with red cheeks.

Walking on the skies as Keats's watcher laughs,
I am an anthropomorphic king, looking down
on the misread feud between Zeus and Fenrir.
The Wolf has broken free of its chains and
Olympus marries Asgard in two private ceremonies.
Awake, I find myself a mere mortal.

Diagonal lines read in slanted motions,
the hellhounds of regret sink their
scripture-ridden teeth deep into vulnerable flesh.
Some have suffered in silence,
but if we open the dog, the dog exposes all.
Awake, I weep in meditation and age eight years in advance.

Astrology enthusiasts beg to be seers in this
century of prolonged numbness, help me not.
If chased by dragons, give back unearthed fortune.
If kissed by a siren, turn away from delusional love illusions.
If blessed by the volcano, let rebirth renew itself in a frenzy
of sharks.
Awake, the twins neck kiss me and away into the morning.

Steady beat after burning lessons learned,
each more titillating than the next.
Oh, let us drink nectar, deliberate failure!
Let her come into my home of souls,
my soul of homes to live in eternal nirvana.
Awake, I laugh off the alternate ending.

Lines that reach the end of infinity's eye,
what will your swan song be?
Elder surrounded by cloud strands, without
a drop of humanity's rain to shed.
A life fulfilled, a glass half full of entire miracles.
Asleep, I count sheeple of society and expect nothing
in return.

FREEZE!

I see you.
I see your lying teeth hovering,
angelic hag of rotten egg eyes,
spoiled milk stench, pungent and thicker than
your skull's remains.
Your splintered cane of pine
burrows deep into my maleficent neck,
releasing Egyptian asps.
Your face looks exactly like I feel,
yet I haven't the strength and willpower
to stand on my own two conscious feet and tell you so.
Leave me be and may your glowing eyes dim all the way.

I see you.
I see your opal eyes of numbness,
staring back at me with unemotional glory.
Lost Grey Alien living among those
who walk Terra's grounds and take them for granted.
Ghost of Dreamer's Past,
you and your oversized cranium
crave my archive of repressed incidents,
crave my vault of rough draft memories.
Your presence stands as still as I feel,
yet I have neither the willower nor care to you so.
Glide in your whirring oval and leave me to grieve the dying
dawn.

I see your silhouette, your outline,
your foul-mouthed demeanor behind your reflective figure.
Shadow Man, you are only but a shadow
when lights provide your ongoing existence.
"I'M GOING TO FUCKING KILL YOU!"
you say in garbled tongues of fiery rage.
Feel your corpse fingers grasping my throat.
Crush not the apple of self-professed identity.
Feel not the sympathy of past victims.

I am one among dozens, eagerly awaiting
your possession ritual before the
darkness doors offer open opportunities.

Freeze!
Die on sight after unsightly encounters
with blackest triad of manipulation.

Freeze!
Elevated heights and maintain springs,
remove me from this conscious realism.
Let my conscience hypnotize me with sweetest head.

Freeze!
...as if I had a choice to lay
upright and view a ceiling of shifting wooden stars.
And angry the fellow who slips in and
out of stitches of time fabric that tomorrow wears.

December 10, 2017

IN THIS GALAXY, WE ARE UNCONSCIOUS PARTICLES

Such events happen after the
evening eyes fall to the inner lids.
Recollection of glances in shyness,
the what ifs, the rejected possibilities, help of gambles and bids.

Unraveling of the tongue's instincts.
Unfurling of the expat flag's holes.
Understanding the nature of the wise.
Neverland is only eight clicks away.
Nevermore a pushing, softhearted mongrel.
Never able to leap past the ability to romanticize.

In this galaxy, we are unconscious particles.
We hover with neither care nor imagination.
In this tome, we are but words for the fools,
making nonsense and adding senses to sensation.

Unwinding of the clock in reversal speech.
Unnecessary party favors amplify her echoes,
Unnerving to find her laughing body in the morning.
Overestimating her power levels in this dream.
Overpowering her estimated strength.
Overjoyed to find a single blood-scribed warning.

In this river, we are unworthy droplets.
We build our own sacred haven.

In this moonrise, we are but incantations,
calling on the sleeping bones of the raven.

Wait for a pulse in crisp cider air,
the environment that surrounds tyrants.
They crave the meat directly in front of blood,
scribbling the consistency of violence.

Around bending sign waves incarnate.
Always forging the ancient signature.
Aiming for the bullet that cannot sway or tempt.
Negating the attacks made by brotherhood.
Negotiating with civilized sentences through sisterhood.
Narrating the omitted words that are supposedly exempt.

In this demonstration, we are clay protesters.
We strive for instantaneous equality.
In this wrecking hull, we are but rebellious rapscallions,
salvaging the most noble refugees.

Strengthened by the weakened state of humanity.
Struggling with blissful bouts of temporary sanity.
Slowly becoming as endangered as Brother Yeti.
Fornicating out of blocked inspiration.
Ejaculating raw elements of creation.
Procreating the century's most operatic libretti.

In this galaxy, we are unconscious particles.
We assume Planet Earth is another hell.

In this bedroom, we are but victims of climax,
dying under the shuddering ecstasy bell.

December 11, 2017

DREAM HORSES AND NIGHT MARES

Thievery in frostbite fields,
blue spotted pony dreamt she could
soar to newfangled heights and
kick off the guardian clouds that followed.
She glides toward the mountaintops that hover over Earth.

Unicorn horn played at the annual
Festival of Elation Evenings,
where all beasts of lore gather to
whinny in a reply of fervor.
To the Bronze Harvest, crops a-plenty,
ripe for the consumption of renewal.
There are no granted wishes, but for the one
of continuous life.

Pegasus, my dearest, fly to the
Greek springs to lap up the transparent elixir
you so desperately crave before an
untimely arena battle between human and myth.
A lyre playing in your honor with the accompaniment of
an operatic aria, ode to the Perseus of a companion.

Black wings engulf the center of all
prior attention spans in the conscious world.
'Tis then when the black stars aligned and
swallowed the parades of pride whole,
obscured by the narrow-minded populace in denial.

The Reaper's steed glowed with crimson eyes,
riding through the crushed and snowy alabaster bone.

December 10, 2017

VARIATIONS ON SELF-INDULGED IMAGERY

Ice stone glistening in Suneye,
child whale watching out of sperm into blue.
Wavering whiskers fall off feline,
off balance, off tone, off key.
Fortunes told devastating forest attacks.
Fire dances to the beat of her distorted moans.

I am shadow.
You are outline.

We waltz to the rhythm of hovering hips,
to the tune of ripe seasonal fruit,
Cake walks to ragtime, rain, dripping falling,
gushing saltwater blood that adapts to sky blue.

Faintest ideas faint after sandpaper
wafts off the rusting caged Moon mouth.
She cannot remember her dying words,
playing on a C harmonica from Germany.
She remembers Bohemian Berlin and the
arts detaching from their mother country.

Her latest sketch melts away and
oozes suburbia's Baroque penmanship.

Subway tubes play backwards routes,
wrong station, upside down timesteps.

Warped views are all they had,
right side up in a green apple kingdom.

Facing freezing faces alone,
the solitudinarian contorts and heaves
misshapen legs to drag on asphalt.

Dragons raise arms not for fight or flight,
but to take notice in majestic beauty above.

Bathe in red and yellow and chuckle at
olden day melodies written for the
subjective audiences not ready to face the truth.
Truth lies in justice, silver-tongued attorney,
silver mane, courtroom underwater,
being judge by river roots rising
towards elevated room above willow trees.

Towers over cowering mongrels without
morals to masticate on, dreaming of Mastodon,
flowing out of thawed suspension,
spreading extinction and mass perplexing looks.

Is there a reason for next year?
Fill out gaps for accidental purposes.
Originally without tusks, burrowing
bones of defense 'neath Stonehenge ground.
This is how a heart breaks, eggshell armor
shackled into place, the prisoner of love

returns to haunt and reclaim prior titles.

So say it,
so be it,
what say you?
Wake up.
Please be you this time.

January 11, 2018

THE BED WHERE NO ONE LAYS

The walls that were scratched by prisoners,
blood of the souls created the words that were woven.
The halls that were built by slaves,
ashes disassembled from bodies of the white omen.

Subservient to no one but themselves,
they only wished for eight hours of peace.
Regaining consciousness, they disregard hallucinations
and dismay.
Like a ship of fools without captain or compass,
wandering aimlessly on majestic seas,
fighting over who slumbers on the bed where no one lays.

Insomniacs to the untrained eye,
the sky has never spread such color.
Flies a falcon that only they can see,
dragging rainbows to the entrance of summer.
Blocked by stonewall gates to the other side,
condemned globe of stone outwits the strength.
"I write because it feels right,"
contemptuous statement from a blind patron saint.

Pinning him against her headboard,
she takes the staff of life as hers.
Running through their heads, circuses of horrors, an
absolute cavalcade.
They can hear the voices of deities

rummage through the pores of exposed flesh,
spreading sensual secrets in between the sheets
of the bed where they laid.

A fated fear walks this direction,
forcing us to find the time to pretend.
Feigning realism is simplicity at its best,
letting ignorance float along the river bend.

They have been asleep throughout the Middle Ages,
winding down after Midas's touch
turns to gold from the misfits inhumane.
They have rolled in the dirt of destitution,
for below the first burial ground
stands the remains of the bed where the dead were slain.

Every colorful sound is a humorous chance,
laughing like two substance-abusing hyenas.
An opportunity for a plunge comes swiftly,
jumping off a cracking dock in the polluted marina.
The altar was reconfigured in time for Beltane,
standing in a ritualistic octagon.
The time for knighted women is now,
hiding below the blanketed mists of Avalon.

A dying breed of humans, caked with
moss and soil rises from below candlelit surfaces.
Just in time for spending dentine winter holidays,
rejuvenation for the ones who speak fire tongues,

rehabilitation for the valleys where they meet.
So, *bona nox* to the two inlovers under the bed
where no one lays.

December 11, 2017

HOPEFUL HOURS, WISHFUL THINKING

Every hour is a written requiem.
Every day is filled with unrequited
personal definitions of L-O-I cannot complete.

I chase her shadow like I
chased inspiration in the days of infancy,
eighteen years of voluntary victimization.
Oh, why can I not find eternal connections?
Forever damned, forever allies.

And in hopeful hours, my candle lights itself,
perspiring wax and parting ways with its old flames.

Tell no pair of ears what transpired here.
Wishful thinking while watching opera in
slow motion and pausing to object the conclusion.
My libretto never measured up to
hers during these ceiling tile counting minutes.

And how I want to lunge forward and
grab the air itself, a worthy substitute
in memory of the absence that I know
is on its way, a cowardly telegram.

Telling candid secrets with myself,
I share a wild tale to make the other me cringe.

This was never an occurrence,
waking up with disappointment.
Never saw her enter my chamber,
outstretched hands until now.

December 10, 2017

OUT OF THE WOMB, INTO THE OUBLIETTE

Lifeless cold inhabitants face another day,
a challenge with purpose in creation.
She miscarried us again, this living woman of tragedy.
Her egg was our only means of salvation.

Which swimmer will wear the flesh crown
when we begin to dream in the deep?
Which martyr will sacrifice himself to
regain the harvest that has yet to be reaped?

The crops were kisses from that wild night.
She married the stone before it called her name.
On a bed of granite they lay and passion to convey.
His surface's crust loved her to the very core.
Memories of dust collect on heir cracked picture frame.
When the stars struck twelve, their heads were led astray.

Hold these signing hands, drift away,
talk with your eyes full of broken glass.
Tame every beast of the field
who wanders on the beds of lemongrass.

A life of luxury in the Crystal Palace
shall never be granted in our vengeful honor.
Call upon the aid of Ms. Feline Bastet.
Send the scribes to write us one last sextet.
Punishing us, we have been sent to the doldrums

of an oubliette.
Blackened hole, see through lightning, we must disintegrate,
our time to forget.

Feeling our way through the echoes of darkness,
we discover one pure spring to share a nightly soak.
In its waters we realize the core of human vitality,
the value of being gentle-hearted folk.

Meditating beyond the point of no turning back,
we find the naked inner being with which we connect.
Encased in gelatinous vulnerability armor,
we discover the gift of touch and the ways to resurrect.

Introducing all members of this grand charade:
Marcus the Traitor, who proudly boasts of battle scars.
Jade, the Lady voluntarily bound to Alastair, his other half.
Griffin, a bumbling army in his window head parade.
Shreta, shapeshifting aeonian feminist to jaguar.
Idolater Brothers, consistently incestuous around their
silver calf.

Remember the Days of Physical Text,
spending our time perusing an eight-story library.
Tomes for all, tome for none,
for this right side up world seems much too contrary.

Philosophical conspiracies, we would consume.
They led us to believe we sealed our fated doom.
Only destination we wanted was safe to assume.

We welcome the poverty of blindness in this cave-turned-bedroom.
We will shed one last tear before carving the family tomb.
The engraving reads, "We have safely returned back into the sacred womb."

December 11, 2017

LAMENT FOR A LONE FALLEN DREAMER

If this to be your predestined end,
from juvenile marionettes and Camel cigarettes,
to cracking muskets and civil bayonets,
let a fare away celebration occur
in your unknown name on this winter's day.

You were always loving the lovers and
betraying the hypocritical fighters.
Speechmaker for the corrupt on autumn dawn shivahs,
traveling with voluntary immigrants on
a newfangled path to the Rainbow Stairway.

A worshiper of candlelight and brother of midnight,
in human life, you had eight names.
Xander on the surface,
Xavier between heartbeats,
Christina on out of body days,
Selena when you were surer,
Vu for creature comforts,
Biko in someone's honor,
Sanath to complete the equation,
Oracle for inquisitive purposes.

As a Dreamer, you were never pleasant in nature,
but we blame you not, crumbling, misshapen puzzle.
Not every piece was found in your series of wars.

Persecution and ejection of saliva was all you knew
on your weakling Earth, victim of circumstance.
They understood not your advancements,
your aspirations while in transition from the
birth body to destiny's change of truth.

Like angels in rebellion, you became
one eighth of the fallen legion.
Purgatorial Dreamland without minds to explain,
second death for deceased worm flesh.

We mourn for your exiled downfall and
sing verses in hopes that your limited vision
will return to our unbiased arms.

Be our professor once more, for we pine away
at your wisdom in polyglot tongues,
reaffirming every ounce of language love.
Let the melting pot of mouths unite as one!

Occupant of every sleeper's terrain,
we sense your infernal struggles from afar,
gliding while feeling reassured on this skyline,
trotting on centaur back on this odd land formation,
diving into the heat of desert mirage oases.

Your soul's sound told us to move forward
with zest and gusto, to remain gung ho
about every presented opportunity.

Still, we smell the acid and breath mints,
exiting your lips and the gums protecting
your chattering white equines, cubed bones.

Still, we conduct a search in continuation
to be recipients of your sanguine smile.

January 12, 2018

DEMISE AND EPITAPH OF THE PLEASANT DREAMERS

Their thickness of wolf's clothing
resolves in the resentment of their own self-loathing.
Their white flag, stained with panicking hands,
forfeiting any further damage to the time sand.
Their screaming gibberish, faces of islands,
igniting the souls beneath the coals, sweetest diamonds.

Trans-skinned soldiers fell to the
alabaster ground, decorating it with battle wounds.
Scars from the previous scrimmage
seeped through uniforms of loyalty on this human
afternoon.

"Alastair, the winding clock has come to an end.
This battle was the predestined obstacle.
This way was the divorce of life and humanity.
Diversity, our assortment of elixir."
On the coast of consciousness, we have lost permission
to ascend.
The Dreamliners have devolved to the mammalian jackals.
Marcus withers away and revokes his own sanity,
a product of metaphysical trial and error.
Laughing into yesterday's dawn,
crying into last evening's dusk.

Shedding the reptilian bodies they possess,
they become bipedal from the flesh-like seams.
Deteriorating and decomposing before the eyes
of the opposition,
they revert to the perspiring tale of lovers
in their dreams.

Marcus, the spirit tiger for real,
roaring to stretch the blissful separation.
Disassembled and reconstructed in the stars,
becoming an immortal on the bridge of constellations.
Out of people's guilty other sides of minds,
into the message of nature's preservation.

Alastair admits to the fault of civil war.
"Only mortal, only human, only lived to please."
Fatal transfer from sea to shining mistake.
His legacy lies in the text of legends, factual folklore.
A mind of sheltered wonders he once was, but he is the heir
to the brains of Sophocles.
Production of the Golden One laid to rest among those
who quake.

Dreamliners scattered throughout the empty temples,
biting their tongues in undead agony.
Leading themselves to water and shoreline scratching
a surface,
plots of land found the others labeling themselves
as enemies.
Forced to roam the hidden corners as beasts,

granting their wish of the servitude after life's matrimony
and beyond.

Pleasant Dreamers split from the quilt,
sharing their common misguided threads.
If their walls could speak slurred speech,
the words would be melodious in between the sheets
of satin beds.
Tales of the Eldest trace back to flashbacks of originality.
Present time conception brings us to a now desolate place
called reality.

December 11, 2017

YOU ARE THE DREAMER, I AM A DREAMER

I am *a* Dreamer,
you are *the* Dreamer.
Seeker of sound truth that makes not a sound,
rising as a slumberous mass without barriers,
falling as a gelatinous mess in love.
Knighted in time, repeated rhymes,
genuine and artificial in one humane body,
inhuman and yet aeonian on seldom occasions.

Lighter of life during peaceful darkness,
stirring chaos into melting pot of diverse unity.
United, we stand, as one soul, we dream.
I am *a* Dreamer,
you are *the* Dreamer.
Entertainer who laughs at any
gaggle of geese landing in wish-making dandelion fields,
for their wishes came to fruition above.

Dialer of the Sun,
Maker of Moon phases,
colonist on Mars's favorite thinking spot,
revolutionary to a rebellious audience.
Lightning bolt thrower with extra privilege,
child without juvenile headspace or brainpower.
I am *a* Dreamer,
you are *the* Dreamer.

I am *a* Dreamer,
you are *the* Dreamers.
Keeper of selective peaceful years,
stoic in nature, but blissful in solitude.
Solipsism left to the self-absorbed river reflection.
Solidarity I never liquidated in this realm,
for we stand as one at all hours of the flying days.
We know not of division and its ramifications.

Feeder of willful prey, sacrificial sensation,
consumer of manna dipped in nectar,
for we have waited forty years, patient as predators.
I am *a* Dreamer,
you are *the* Dreamers.
Shaking and moving in high society, the match is thrown
on the clothes of gasoline.
Drinker of pure waters,
bathing in the lukewarm content that blesses utopian
existence.

Singer of self-penned verses,
poet only for Her muse-like tendencies,
semi-traditionalist for the folk without backbones.
Artist for every naked canvas lacking shame,
mythology enthusiast for the commonwealth of none,
bibliophile beyond the time of scented elderly books.
I am *a* Dreamer,
you are *the* Dreamers.

January 13, 2018

Z. M. Wise is a proud Illinois native from the Northwest Suburbs of Chicago, poet, vocalist/ lyricist/ songwriter, essayist, occasional playwright, seldom screenwriter, co-editor and arts activist, writing since his first steps as a child. He was selected to be a performer in the Word Around Town Tour in 2013, a Houston citywide tour. He is co-owner and co-editor of Transcendent Zero Press, an independent publishing house for poetry that produces an international quarterly journal known as Harbinger Asylum. The journal was nominated Best Poetry Journal in 2013 at the National Poetry Awards.

He is the author of eight books and chapbooks of published poetry, as well as a play. Other than these books, his poems, lyrics, essays, and book reviews have been published in various journals, magazines, and anthologies. The motto that keeps him going: POETRY LIVES AND LONG LIVE THE ARTS! Mr. Wise will make sure to spread that message and the love of the arts, making sure it remains vibrant for the rest of his days and beyond. Besides poetry and other forms of writing, his other passions/interests include playing a few instruments, creative & professional voice acting, creating visual art, cooking/baking, fitness, and reading.

OTHER BOOKS

Poetry (Chapbooks)

The Nightmare Mask (Weasel Press, 2022)
Kosmish and the Horned Ones (Weasel Press, 2018)
Cuentos de Amor (Red Ferret Press, 2015)

Poetry (Full-Length Collections)

Illinois Infinitarium (Cherry House Press, 2020)
Wolf: An Epic and Other Poems (Weasel Press, 2015)
The Wandering Poet (Transcendent Zero Press, 2014)
Take Me Back, Kingswood Clock! (MavLit Press, 2013, out of print)

Play:

Bottles of Emerald for the Demon Queen (Transcendent Zero Press, 2019)

CIP - Каталогизација у публикацији
Народна библиотека Србије, Београд

821.131.1-1

Z. M. Wise
The Pleasant Dreamers: A Nonlinear Epic / Z. M. Wise; [engleski jezik]. – 1. izd. – Beograd : Sunčani breg, 2023. – 99 str; 21 cm. – (Biblioteka Poezija; knj. 31). Tiraž: 200. – beleška o autoru: str. 97.

ISBN 978-86-7974-773-0
COBISS.SR-ID 283414028